FRANK LLOYD WRIGHT

By Gretchen Will Mayo

WORLD ALMANAC® LIBRARY

Please visit our web site at: www.worldalmanaclibrary.com
For a free color catalog describing World Almanac® Library's list
of high-quality books and multimedia programs, call 1-800-848-2928 (USA)
or 1-800-387-3178 (Canada). World Almanac® Library's fax: (414) 332-3567.

Library of Congress Cataloging-in-Publication Data

Mayo, Gretchen.
    Frank Lloyd Wright / by Gretchen Will Mayo.
      p. cm. — (Trailblazers of the modern world)
    Includes bibliographical references and index.
    Summary: Examines the life and career of the American architect, detailing the evolution of his innovative
design and the structures which won him fame around the world.
    ISBN 0-8368-5101-3 (lib. bdg.)
    ISBN 0-8368-5261-3 (softcover)
    1. Wright, Frank Lloyd, 1867-1959—Juvenile literature. 2. Architects—United States—Biography—
Juvenile literature. [1. Wright, Frank Lloyd, 1867-1959. 2. Architects.] I. Title. II. Series.
  NA737.W7M34   2004
  720'.92—dc22
  [B]   2003065365

First published in 2004 by
World Almanac® Library
330 West Olive Street, Suite 100
Milwaukee, WI 53212 USA

Copyright © 2004 by World Almanac® Library.

Project manager: Jonny Brown
Editor: Jim Mezzanotte
Design and page production: Scott M. Krall
Photo research: Diane Laska-Swanke
Indexer: Walter Kronenberg

Photo credits: © AP/Wide World Photos: 4 top, 41 top; Catherine Tobin Wright (b.1871 - d.1959) c. unknown,
Photographer: unknown. Collection of Frank Lloyd Wright Preservation Trust, H&S H212.: 19; Catherine Tobin
Wright and Wright children portraits (Frank Lloyd Wright's first wife and their children) c. 1909, Photographer:
unknown. Collection of Frank Lloyd Wright Preservation Trust, H&S H 254.: 26; © CORBIS: 15; © Sandy
Felsenthal/CORBIS: 25; Frank Lloyd Wright and his family on the front stairs of Oak Park, Illinois home,
c. 1890, Photographer: unknown. Collection of Frank Lloyd Wright Preservation Trust, H&S H 92.: 14;
Courtesy The Frank Lloyd Wright Archives, Scottsdale, AZ: 4 bottom, 6 both, 8 both, 9, 11, 13, 17, 20, 23, 24, 28,
31, 32, 33, 35, 36 bottom, 37, 40, 41 bottom; © Farrell Grehan/CORBIS: 7, 36 top; © Hulton Archive/Getty Images:
cover, 18; © Catherine Karnow/CORBIS: 42; © JoAnn Early Macken: 39; © David Samuel Robbins/CORBIS: 5;
© Michael Rougier/Time Life Pictures/Getty Images: 43

Printed in the United States of America

1 2 3 4 5 6 7 8 9 08 07 06 05 04

TABLE of CONTENTS

Words that appear in the glossary are printed in **boldface**
type the first time they occur in the text.

CHAPTER 1

THE VISION OF A GENIUS

Frank Lloyd Wright (above, left) with a model of his design for the Guggenheim Museum in New York City (below)

When you enter a building, do you stop to think who designed it? Architects—the people who design the buildings we inhabit—sometimes don't get much recognition for what they create. There are many famous buildings in the world, but the architects who design them often remain relatively unknown.

Frank Lloyd Wright, however, became a celebrity in his lifetime, and for good reason. Today, Wright is considered the greatest of American architects. Working as an architect for an amazingly full seventy-two years, he designed 1,141 buildings, including houses, offices, churches, schools, and libraries. His brilliant ideas about architecture revolutionized the way houses and other buildings were designed and constructed.

ARCHITECTURE FOR A CHANGING WORLD

When Wright was born, in 1867, only two years had passed since the end of the Civil War. Neither the telephone nor the electric light bulb had been invented, and automobiles were nonexistent. Most people believed human flight was impossible. By the time Wright died, however, in 1959, space exploration had begun. Technological advances in transportation, communications, and other fields had transformed the way people lived.

In many ways, this period of change and innovation is reflected in the buildings Wright created. His designs were a departure from the architectural traditions of the past, and he constantly sought to redefine the environments in which people lived and worked. For Wright, a building provided more than just shelter and comfort—it helped shape the lives of its inhabitants. As he once said, "A building is not just a place to be. It is a way to be."

Wright hated the multi-storied, **Victorian**-style homes that were popular in his early years, calling their closed-off rooms boxes inside boxes. He created interiors with an open flow of space, and his houses often had no walls to separate living and dining rooms. Wright also found ways to allow people who lived and worked inside his buildings to have a sense that they were connected to the natural world outside their walls.

When Wright began working as an architect in the 1880s, Victorian-style houses—which featured fancy, ornate woodwork, multiple stories, and many rooms—were very popular.

RESPECT FOR NATURE

A captivating speaker, teacher, and writer, Wright often preached the beauty of nature, as well as his belief that buildings should be an integral part of their natural surroundings. He urged other architects to rely on the natural beauty of wood, brick, and stone. Nature's influence is apparent in the clean, horizontal lines of his houses, which hug rather than dominate the landscape. The patterns of nature can also be found in the various fabrics, furniture, stained glass, lamps, dinnerware, stonework, and **graphic arts** that Wright designed.

Belonging to a Hill

In his **autobiography**, Frank Lloyd Wright said, "I knew well that no house should ever be on a hill or on anything. It should be of the hill. Belonging to it. Hill and house should live together each the happier for the other."

Like many Wright designs, this 1902 house features clean, horizontal lines that help it blend in with the landscape.

Wright expressed his creative vision in even the smallest details, such as the patterns used in these stained glass windows in the 1910 Robie House.

A GIFTED BUT COMPLEX MAN

Although Wright's extraordinary imagination fueled an outpouring of highly creative designs, many of his buildings were never constructed. He lost some clients because of the many scandals in his personal life. But he also lost clients because he ignored their wishes and concerns. Wright earned a well-deserved reputation for creating huge cost overruns on his projects.

Nevertheless, many who recognized Wright's genius hired him. His **commissions** often came from the wealthy, whom he courted with the instincts of a born salesman. Wright made good use of his outgoing personality, and he could be charming. He was extremely well read, he studied the arts and music, and he loved automobiles. His wide-ranging interests led to many valuable friendships.

Frank Wright's arrogance and legendary self-indulgences damaged many of his relationships, both personal and professional. But despite his faults, there is no denying his tireless ambition to create buildings that would enhance people's lives. He faced personal tragedy, financial hardship, harsh criticism, and professional ridicule. Yet he stuck to his unique architectural ideas.

Today, Frank Lloyd Wright is called "the Father of American Architecture." He showed the world that a building ought to fit its natural surroundings and the needs of its inhabitants. In the last hundred years, many elements of Wright's architectural style have had a huge influence on home design across the United States. Tourists and students from all over the world travel to view and study Wright-designed buildings. Wright might have been born in a bygone era, but the importance of his architecture continues to be felt in the twentieth-first century, and many of his ideas are as fresh and inspirational as ever.

The Monona Terrace Convention Center in Madison, Wisconsin. The construction of this Wright-designed building began in 1994, more than thirty years after the architect's death (see page 43).

CHAPTER 2

SHAPING A BOY'S TALENTS

Anna Lloyd Wright

William Wright

Frank Lloyd Wright was born on June 7, 1867, in Richland Center, a small town in Wisconsin. His mother, Anna Lloyd Jones, was a former schoolteacher. His father, William C. Wright, was a lawyer, minister, and musician.

When Anna married William, she was twenty-eight years old. At age six she had come from Wales to the United States with her family. They and other relatives settled on farms near Spring Green, Wisconsin. Anna's close-knit family belonged to a liberal, free-thinking Christian group that preached "the unity of all things" and became known as the Unitarians. Family members were fiercely loyal to one another. They always felt that they were outsiders who stood alone for right thinking. Their motto was "Truth against the World."

Anna was William Wright's second wife. His first wife had died. When he met Anna, he was forty-one years old. William was handsome, smart, and outgoing. He had gone to college at age fourteen and earned a law degree. Then he became an ordained minister. He was a gifted speaker, singer, violinist, pianist, organist, and composer, and people were drawn to him because of his talents and personality.

FAMILY TENSIONS

Despite William's many talents, however, he struggled to support his family. He seldom practiced law. Instead, he moved his family to the various places where he preached. He earned little or no money, and he was disastrously bad at managing the family's finances. The family, meanwhile, kept growing. Anna had already become stepmother to William's three children by his first wife. Then, less than a year after the couple was married, Frank was born, and he was soon followed by two younger sisters, Jane and Maginel. The headstrong, ambitious Anna probably found William to be a terrible disappointment. She resented living in poverty, and she was often particularly abusive toward her stepdaughter Elizabeth.

As her dreams of an easier life faded, Anna focused much of her attentions on her only son Frank. Still a teacher at heart, she became interested in the work of Friedrich Froebel, a pioneer in the study of early childhood development. Froebel, who started the world's first kindergarten, believed that children should be encouraged in their talents at an early age. Anna believed that architecture—the designing and building of structures—would be an excellent profession for Frank to pursue. At the time, architecture did not have the status it enjoys today, and many architects were just former builders who created their own designs. But Anna sought to instill a passion for architecture in her young son. In his autobiography, Wright commented, "I had grown up from childhood with the idea that there was nothing quite so sacrosanct, so high, so sacred as an architect, a builder."

When Frank was nine years old, Anna gave him a gift of wooden blocks. By joining the various blocks in

Frank Lloyd Wright, about age two

different combinations, Frank learned that all structures, no matter how big or complex, are made of basic geometric shapes, such as squares, rectangles, and triangles. Even late in life, Frank said, "The smooth cardboard triangles and Maplewood blocks . . . are in my fingers to this day."

William was aware that Anna pampered Frank. To compensate, he was strict with the boy, never letting Frank get away with bad behavior. In this way, Frank's upbringing was inconsistent, being either too lenient or too rigid. By age ten, he was already a master at avoiding issues or arguing his way out of blame or punishment.

SETTLING IN WISCONSIN

William's ministry work eventually took the Wright family out of state, but he moved the family back to Wisconsin when Frank was ten years old. The Wright family settled in Madison, the state capital, which is located on a strip of land separating Lake Mendota from Lake Monona. William decided to open a music school. He and Anna were soon able to buy a house on the shore of Lake Mendota, only eight blocks from the capitol building.

To increase his income, William sold popular music that he composed. His children often saw him composing at the family piano, with a pen clenched between his teeth dripping ink on his white beard. Late into the night, Frank would hear his father playing the piano or violin, and over time he memorized long stretches of Beethoven's symphonies and other great musical works. Taught by his father, Frank became a skilled pianist and violist, and he developed a lifelong love for music.

Frank was an avid reader and spent many hours with his father's extensive book collection. The story he enjoyed most, and always remembered, was about Aladdin and his magic lamp from the book *The Arabian Nights*. Smart, resourceful Aladdin was able to triumph over every obstacle with the help of his magic lamp. Frank might have imagined himself as Aladdin. He might have believed that Aladdin's lamp was a symbol for creativity—a gift that could solve all problems.

SHAGGY TO THE RESCUE

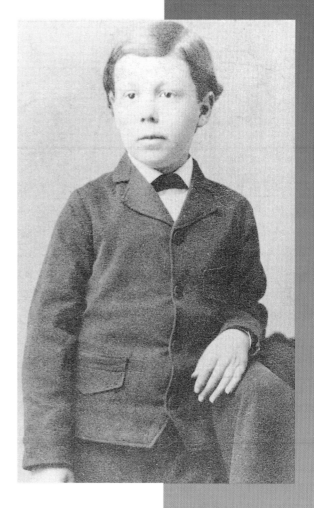

Frank Wright, age ten

In seventh and eighth grades at Madison's Second Ward School, classmates nicknamed Frank "Shaggy" for his long hair. Perhaps because his family had moved so often, Frank earned poor to average grades and mostly kept to himself. When Frank was twelve, however, he came to the rescue of Robie Lamp, a thirteen-year-old boy who had been crippled by a childhood illness. Other boys grabbed Robie's crutches and threw him to the ground, but Frank chased the boys away. Robie became Frank's lifelong friend.

Both boys were bright and inventive, and they loved to draw and make designs. They played on the two lakes in Madison, and from salvaged materials they built a paddle boat, bows and arrows, kites, a catamaran, and a double-runnered bobsled. At the time, ice boats were in fashion. These sleek, newfangled vehicles used sail power to skate across the frozen surfaces of lakes, and they could be seen in winter speeding back and forth on Lake Mendota, close to the Wrights' home. The boys built their own ice boat.

In the Wrights' basement, the boys also learned to print business and calling cards on Frank's small printing press. They soon longed for a larger press, but they couldn't afford one. Frank asked a wealthy neighbor, Mr. Doyon, to lend them $200. The man agreed to provide the loan, but only if his son Charlie was included. Frank, Robie, and Charlie Doyon formed a company called Wright, Doyon, and Lamp, Publishers and Printers. Mr. Doyon became the first of many wealthy patrons who would help Frank Wright during his life, and Frank began a lifelong interest in graphic arts.

FARMING AND FAMILY

Anna Wright might have pampered her son, but every year, from the time Frank was eleven to the time he was sixteen, she sent Frank to help her brother on his farm near Spring Green, Wisconsin. Frank's uncle James was a hard taskmaster, and Frank complained bitterly about the endless, backbreaking farm chores. His uncle told him, "add tired to tired," and wouldn't let him wriggle out of work. "Work is an

Patterns on the Farm

Frank Lloyd Wright designed every one of his buildings around repeated geometric shapes, creating a feeling of unity throughout the structure. As a boy, he discovered the beauty of repetitious patterns when performing tedious work on his uncle's farm. His repeated movements while pitching hay or planting corn suggested a musical beat, and he invented rhythmic songs as he squirted cow's milk into a pail. Wright observed visual patterns in corn rows, rocks, and ripples in the streams. "More significant than all else at this time," Wright later recalled, "was this sense of rhythm."

A photo of Spring Green, Wisconsin, taken by Frank Wright

adventure that makes strong men and finishes weak ones," he said.

On Sundays at his uncle's farm, Frank scrubbed off the field dirt, put on his Sunday-best city clothes, and went to family religious services. Uncle Jenkin Lloyd-Jones was the preacher. Afterward the Lloyd-Jones clan often had picnics, and Frank was free to join in the singing or listen to stories. Decades later, he tried to recreate these happy gatherings of his childhood when he opened his school for architects.

A LESSON FOR THE FUTURE

On November 8, 1883, when Frank was a sixteen-year-old junior attending class at Madison High School, the center of the nearby Capitol building's new south wing collapsed with a crashing roar. Rushing to Capitol Square, Frank witnessed a horrifying scene. Eight workmen were dead, and sixteen were seriously injured. The architect was blamed for design flaws and poor supervision of the project. The contractor had filled support columns with inferior material, and the iron sup-

A photo of Frank Wright (seated, far right) and family, circa 1890. From left: Frank's uncle, Jenkin Lloyd-Jones, and his aunt, Susan Lloyd-Jones; his sister, Jane; his wife, Catherine, and their son, Lloyd; his mother, Anna; his sister, Maginel; and his cousin, Mary.

plier had provided defective columns. Their **negligence** horrified Frank and greatly influenced his resolve, later in life, to design safe buildings.

LIFE TAKES A TURN

About this time, Frank realized that his parents' marriage was crumbling. As arguments over money increased, their relationship became worse. Anna told William she hated him, and she even attacked him physically. In December 1884, William filed for divorce. The divorce agreement left him with only his clothes, his violins, some books, and a mahogany bookcase. It's doubtful that Frank Wright ever saw his father again.

With William gone, only Frank and his two younger sisters remained at home with Anna. Seventeen years old and a senior in high school, Frank had now become the "man of the house." It was his responsibility to support the family.

"Agonized Cries"

In his autobiography, Wright recalled what he saw after the collapse of the Capitol building in Madison. "A cloud of white **lime** dust . . . from the windows of the [capitol's] outside walls" were followed by "agonized human cries." Workers escaping from the basement and covered with lime dust and blood tried to throw off chunks of masonry and beams. "Some fell dead on the grass under the clear sky and others fell insensible." Frank saw one moaning worker hanging upside down from a windowsill, his foot crushed and pinned by an iron beam. "A ghastly red stream ran from him down the stone wall." Then someone noticed a man's hand sticking out from the debris. Rescuers threw bricks aside to retrieve the crushed, lifeless body. Wright watched for hours. Finally, he went home ill and "dreamed of it that night and the next and the next."

Frank Wright needed a job—fast. Allan Conover, a respected engineer and architect as well as a professor at the University of Wisconsin, had an office not far from where William Wright had taught music. Conover hired Frank as an office helper in 1886.

In addition to working for Conover, Frank became a part-time student at the University of Wisconsin in Madison. He took courses in French, mechanical drawing, and descriptive geometry. It was Frank's experiences with Conover, however, that probably had the most impact on the young man. His goal of becoming an architect became firmly set.

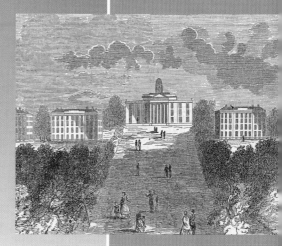

An 1851 illustration of the University of Wisconsin campus in Madison, Wisconsin

Life Lessons from an Extraordinary Teacher

Frank Lloyd Wright claimed that he learned everything on his own, which helped earn him a reputation for being arrogant. But he admitted that his job with Professor Conover was "a great good" and "the work was truly educational."

Allan Conover was exactly the right teacher for the budding architectural genius, for several reasons. First, Conover was keenly interested in new technology. Second, while other engineering professors taught from dry military textbooks, Conover took his students and apprentices to actual building projects in the field, asking for their solutions to municipal problems. Last, Conover **delegated** difficult tasks, even to his young employees. At a construction site in winter, for example, he sent Frank Wright to the top of a skeleton of steel **girders** to remove a faulty piece of equipment.

FRANK STEPS OUT

Except for geometry, Frank didn't like his university courses. He was much more interested in campus social life. Frank had previously thought of himself as shy and awkward among strangers, especially girls, but he began to reinvent himself. He joined a fraternity, which probably cost as much as his **tuition** and books, and he sang bass in the University Choral Club. Although he had no money, he charged fancy new clothing at stores. Once he rented a horse-drawn carriage to take a date to a party that was less than a block from her dormitory.

The young man's work with Conover fueled his dreams. Frank longed to be wealthy and important. Although he was only eighteen, he already thought of himself as an architect. When his uncle, Jenkin Lloyd-Jones, urged the family congregation to build a Unitarian chapel near Spring Green, Frank sent his uncle designs and a letter proposing that he be hired as architect. Frank's uncle, however, had already planned for a renowned Chicago architect, J. L. Silsbee, to design the chapel.

Frank became convinced that Chicago was the place to make a name for himself. In early 1887, he secretly left the Wrights' home on Lake Mendota and took a train to Chicago. To purchase his one-way ticket, Frank sold some of his family's most valuable books, as well as his mother's **mink** collar, to a Madison **pawn shop**.

A BIG BREAK IN THE BIG CITY

Chicago was growing rapidly, but one architectural firm after another refused Frank a job. He was soon out of money and tired of eating bananas. Finally, he applied at the office of J. L. Silsbee. Although Silsbee was now designing the new All Souls' Church in Chicago, where Frank's uncle, Jenkin Lloyd-Jones, had become the minister, Frank didn't mention this family connection to Silsbee. Frank was hired on his own merit.

Silsbee specialized in designing elegant, traditional houses. Frank admired Silsbee's "soft, deep black lead pencil strokes" and his "remarkable free-hand sketches," and he tried to achieve the same curving flow of forms. But he grew impatient drawing pretty houses to impress Silsbee's clients. "The buildings he constructs never look like the pictures," Frank complained to Cecil Corwin, a Silsbee draftsman. Cecil replied that practical architects built what the clients asked. "That's not honest," Frank answered. "Each man must do the best he knows how to do, and not just what he is told to do."

Frank had arrived in Chicago with little money and few connections, but he did possess some important traits that helped him get ahead. He was a hard worker, and he made use of every opportunity to improve his skills. He also had a knack for making important people feel they should help him. Despite his outward confidence, he secretly feared that his lack of wealth and formal training might get in the way of his success. But this fear actually caused him to push harder than others.

Although Frank Wright worked only one year for the Silsbee firm, he learned a great deal and made influential friends. He also grew to appreciate

"A Pattern of Behavior"

At Silsbee's office, Wright quickly made friends with Cecil Corwin, who invited Frank to dinner, offered Frank a room in his house, and even lent Frank money. Frank explained he needed ten dollars (more than a week's wages) to send to his mother and would repay it two dollars at a time. In his autobiography, Wright admitted, "A pattern of behavior had begun." Throughout life, he often asked friends for loans.

Frank Lloyd Wright

Silsbee's Japanese art collection. But Wright wanted to earn more money and work with less traditional forms of architecture than Silsbee's Victorian homes. When he heard of a project opening at the very prestigious firm of Adler and Sullivan, he applied. Wright was hired just as Louis Sullivan was about to make a great breakthrough. Under Sullivan's direction, the modern skyscraper would be born. Louis Sullivan would become a towering figure in the field of American architecture and a mentor to Frank Lloyd Wright.

Louis Henri Sullivan, circa 1890. Creating tall, steel-framed buildings, Sullivan helped usher in the age of the modern skyscraper. His work had a huge influence on American architecture in the twentieth century.

CATHERINE

Through his uncle Jenkin's Chicago church, as well as through new friends he had made, the young, single Wright had plenty of opportunities to socialize with women. But one social encounter happened quite by accident. One night, while dancing at a costume party, Frank and a pretty stranger crashed heads and fell in a heap. Catherine Tobin had blue eyes and curly red hair. She was a tall, sixteen-year-old high school student whom Wright described as "gay-spirited" and "sunny-haired," with "a frank, handsome" face. He wasted no time in asking for a date. Before long, Frank Wright was regularly eating Sunday dinner with the Tobin family. He and Catherine had fallen in love.

Anna Wright had forgiven Frank for sneaking away to Chicago, but she was not happy to hear that her only son, whom she still considered to be the "man of the house," was getting married. She traveled to Chicago to talk him out of his plans. When Frank refused to change his mind, Anna and her two daughters, Jane and

Maginel, moved to Oak Park, a suburb of Chicago. Frank moved in with them, but only for a brief time. Despite Anna's arguments, Frank went ahead with his wedding plans, and on June 1, 1889, he and Catherine were married.

DREAMS COME TRUE

Catherine Tobin Wright

In his autobiography, Wright recalled that he returned from his honeymoon with a proposition for Sullivan. "If you want me to work for you as long as five years," Wright asked, "couldn't you lend me enough money to build a little house and let me pay you back so much each month, taken out of my pay envelope?"

Louis Sullivan agreed to the proposition, immediately giving Wright $5,000—a very large sum of money at that time—for a five-year work contract. This kind of commitment to an employee was highly unusual. But Sullivan wanted to keep Frank in the firm because he demonstrated an exceptional ability to imagine three-dimensional space and quickly come up with problem-solving ideas for clients' projects.

The money, however, came with a warning. "Now look out," Sullivan said to Frank. "I know your tastes . . . no extras."

Wright agreed. But as Wright recalled, when the house was almost complete, "There was $1,200 more to be paid . . . I kept this in the dark, paid in due course as I could of what remained of my salary or I could earn overtime."

Sullivan made Wright his chief assistant, then chief designer specializing in houses. Frank Wright oversaw thirty draftsmen.

Less than three years had passed since Wright left Madison. He was working for one of the most respected architects in the United States, he was married to the lovely Catherine Tobin, and he lived in a beautiful house, which he had designed, in one of the best suburbs of Chicago. Frank Lloyd Wright was only twenty-two years old.

The Wright home in Oak Park. Wright used his residence as a place to experiment with new ideas, so it was constantly changing. He added a studio to the house in 1898.

THE BEST OF EVERYTHING

Frank and Catherine Wright had two children in just a few years, and their growing family strained their finances. But Wright still wanted only the best of everything—rugs, clothing, a camera, a horse, entertainment. His attitude was exactly opposite that of most people. "So long as we had the luxuries, the necessities could pretty well take care of themselves," he said.

Wright was spending more than he earned, just as he'd done when he was a college boy. Needing money, he began to **moonlight**, designing houses for people who weren't clients of Adler and Sullivan. Wright had to hide his work from Sullivan, so when the designs were published he used Cecil Corwin's name instead of his own. Sullivan found out about the moonlighting, however, and was angry. In 1893, Sullivan fired Wright, although Wright had a year left on his contract. Wright neither saw nor talked to his revered mentor for twelve years.

ON HIS OWN

The Wrights were expecting their third child, and Frank was unemployed. Bills piled up, both for family essentials and for the luxuries Frank craved. Now twenty-six, Wright opened his own architectural office and began his solo career by entering two design contests. He won the first, a $7,000 commission for two boathouses in Madison.

Although Wright did not win the second contest, his entry caught the eye of Daniel Burnham, the newly elected president of the American Institute of Architects. Amazed by Wright's grasp of **classical** European architecture, Burnham made an astonishing offer. He would pay all of Frank's expenses for four years of architectural study in France, followed by two more years in Rome. In return, Frank would work for Burnham.

BIG AMBITIONS

Only a year before, Wright would have leaped at Burnham's offer. But Wright turned it down because he had a more ambitious goal. His work over the past five years had led him away from classical, European building styles. To Wright's way of thinking, multi-storied houses, which separated people in boxlike rooms, were not the living spaces that families needed. Frank wanted to develop a new form of architecture that he believed was much better suited to the American Midwest and its people.

THE PRAIRIE STYLE

Other young American architects also wanted to break away from tradition. Wright became their leader in a powerful new design philosophy that became known as the Prairie Style, which got its name from the **prairies** of the Midwest.

Wright wrote and gave lectures about the Prairie Style, and he established a set of characteristics to define it:

- Buildings should blend in with nature, not dominate it.

- Materials natural to an area, such as native woods and stone, should be used.

- The space designed should offer both a sheltering hearth and a sense of unity with nature outdoors.

- Living spaces should be flexible and open.

- Nature should inspire the decorations, and interior ornamentation should be kept to a minimum.

- Industrial-age resources, such as steel beams and reinforced concrete, should be used in ways that make spaces more beautiful and inspiring.

- Exteriors of Prairie Style houses should reflect the prairie's horizontal lines.

- Furniture, art glass windows, and lighting fixtures should be built to create a sense of unity throughout.

BREAKTHROUGH DESIGNS

Developing his architectural style, Wright experimented with rooflines, roof overhangs, and windows grouped in horizontal bands. Then, between 1900 and 1909, Wright poured out a flood of highly original home designs that brought him much fame. Most of his clients were well-educated professionals who weren't afraid of new ideas. Darwin D. Martin was one of them.

Martin was the chief executive of the Larkin Company, a national manufacturer of soaps, perfumes, and powders. When the company needed a new administration building in Buffalo, New York, Martin hired Wright to design it. For Wright, the Larkin project was an important entry into the world of large building commissions, and it gained worldwide attention when it was completed.

FORM AND FUNCTION

The site for the new Larkin building was in a busy industrial area, so Wright designed the outside of the building to be a fortress against the noise and air pollution. But **skylights** lit the stunning interior court, which rose up five stories and was ringed by tiers of balconies. Wright introduced many technical innovations in the design, such as central heating and a form of air conditioning that used blocks of ice. He united form (the elements of his design) with function (the purpose of the building and the needs

Designs With a Twist

During Wright's first years on his own as an architect, most of his commissions were for private homes. Although he tried to satisfy his clients' wishes for popular, traditional styles, he gave each design an unusual twist. The Winslow House, for example, built in River Forest, Illinois, in 1894, had a flattened, elongated roof that seemed to float over the house. This innovation was considered quite radical at the time, and it caused quite a stir in suburban Chicago. In fact, the house's owner, William Winslow, took the back road to the commuter train to avoid his ridiculing neighbors. Nevertheless, some respected critics of architecture praised Wright as a bright new star.

The Winslow House

of its inhabitants), creating a useful workspace that was also attractive and comfortable for employees.

Wright worked to combine form with function in his house plans, too. In 1906, Frederick C. Robie, a prosperous young bicycle manufacturer, came to Wright's office with precise needs for a new house in Chicago. It had to be fireproof, with separate quarters for his children that included a walled garden to keep them from wandering. The living room had to allow him to look up and down the street without being seen by the neighbors. Robie's requests might have been unusual, but they were perfectly suited to Wright's architecture. The finished house, with its wide, cantilevered roof overhang, stands today like a grand brick boat that could sail across the prairie. Robie House is widely considered one of the best examples of Frank Lloyd Wright's Prairie Style designs.

Robie House. Note the house's horizontal lines and wide roof overhangs, which are supported by steel cantilevers. The house is now a Historic National Landmark.

WRIGHT'S USE OF THE CANTILEVER

Many of Wright's buildings had roofs that extended far beyond the exterior walls. These innovative overhangs shaded rooms during the summer but allowed sunlight to enter during winter months. Wright had to assure skeptical clients that the overhangs, which had no support beneath them, would not collapse. He had designed the roofs, he told his clients, with cantilevers.

A cantilever is a horizontal beam or structure that is supported on only one end (or in the middle) but can still support weight at its other end. Wright understood that a strong, rigid cantilever, like the thick branch of a tree, could support a great amount of weight at its free end. Wright featured cantilevers, which were often made of steel or reinforced concrete, in many of his designs. He used cantilevers to make roof overhangs, balconies, and even whole rooms appear to be floating above the ground with no vertical support.

THE PRICE OF SUCCESS

Between 1893 and 1909, Frank Wright received about 430 commissions. Of these designs, approximately 130 were built. This huge output would have been a lifetime's work for most architects.

Some of Wright's innovations were controversial. His plan for the Unitarian church's Unity Temple in Oak Park, for example, called for concrete construction to prevent fire and keep out noise from the busy street. It would be one of the first buildings constructed of concrete. Wright had to prepare a model to convince church members his revolutionary ideas were worthy of a church. When finished, Unity Temple was criticized, despite its peaceful and lovely interior. To many people, using concrete to build a church was **sacrilege**.

By 1909, Wright was one of the most famous architects in the United States. His architectural work had been celebrated twice in exhibitions at the Art Institute of Chicago, and at least ninety-six articles about his work had appeared in popular and professional magazines.

For sixteen years, Wright had thrown himself into his work, leaving Catherine to raise the children—they now had six—

The interior of the Unity Temple. Note the high placement of windows, which allows light to enter while still maintaining privacy.

and tend to the house. He and Catherine had grown apart. Wright felt burned out. He wanted to escape from his work, family, and wife. He asked Catherine for a divorce, but she refused, believing that he would change his mind.

Portraits of Catherine Tobin Wright (bottom, right) and the Wright children, circa 1909. Clockwise from top left: David Samuel; Catherine; John Kenneth; Frank Lloyd, Jr.; Frances; and Robert Llewellyn.

In September 1909, Wright left Oak Park to travel to Europe. He was joined there by Mamah Borthwick Cheney, the wife of a former client. They stayed abroad for months. When Wright returned to Oak Park, Catherine and the children welcomed him home. But Wright was secretly planning for a fresh start in life—including a new house.

"I wished to be a part of my beloved southern Wisconsin," Wright recalled later. "I wanted a natural house to live in myself. . . . Nothing at all I had ever seen would do." Wright "scanned the hills of the region around Spring Green where rock came cropping out in a **strata** to suggest buildings." He imagined a house surrounded by a farm, everything from apple trees in bloom on the hill to grazing Holstein cows. Wright borrowed $25,000 from his old client Darwin Martin, telling Martin that he needed the money to restart his architecture practice. Then he used the money to build a new home. He named it Taliesin, after a hero in **Welsh** myth.

Construction of Taliesin, located near Spring Green, began in May of 1911. Mamah, newly divorced, moved into the building with Wright in August, before it was even completed. Frank Wright was still married to Catherine. His affair with Mamah was highly unusual for the times and considered absolutely immoral. But Wright seemed blind to the effect it would have on his career.

December headlines in *The Chicago Tribune* broadcast the couple's shocking behavior. As word traveled across the country, Wright's potential clients began to vanish. No one wanted to hire a man so tainted by scandal.

A HORRIBLE TRAGEDY

On Saturday, August 14, 1914, Wright was in Chicago working on a project when he received a phone message that Taliesin was in flames. Rushing to Spring Green, Wright found Taliesin in smoldering ruins. But more than the building had been destroyed. Mamah, her two visiting children, and four workers were dead.

Wright learned that Julian Carlton, a handyman at Taliesin, had poured gasoline through various rooms while residents and workers were eating lunch. The crazed man set the gasoline afire, then savagely attacked Mamah with a hatchet. Carlton tried to kill anyone, including the children, who attempted to escape the fire. Only two of those who were eating lunch that day escaped death.

After burying Mamah, Wright hoped that a return to Chicago might take his mind off the horror he had experienced at Taliesin. Preferring to roam among strangers, he walked the streets of Chicago for days, his mind numbed by grief.

CHAPTER 5

TURMOIL AND SUCCESS

rank Lloyd Wright was devastated by the tragedy at Taliesin. Throughout his life, however, Wright found an energizing force in his work that snapped him back when he was at his lowest. Wright believed that work should be "the creative and joyful essence of daily life." In 1914, at the age of forty-seven, he began rebuilding Taliesin, creating a structure that was even more spectacular than before.

A NEW ROMANCE

Not long after the Taliesin tragedy, a new woman entered Wright's life. Miriam Noel, a beautiful socialite who was also a sculptor, began her relationship with Wright by sending a letter of sympathy after the fire. She believed she was destined to have a legendary romance with Wright. She called Wright "Lord of my Waking Dreams."

Frank Wright at his drafting table, circa the mid-1920s

Wright couldn't resist Miriam's flattery. The couple moved into the remains of Taliesin together, and Wright forged ahead with the grand rebuilding. When his sister Maginel visited, she found twenty-five men hard at work. Wright spared no expense in the reconstruction. Again, the architect thought more about his ideas than about cost.

OFF TO JAPAN

In 1916, when Wright was desperate for money, he was given the opportunity of a lifetime. The Japanese government chose him to design the new Imperial Hotel in Tokyo, as well as oversee its construction. That year, he left for Japan, with Miriam in tow, for a project that would not be completed until 1922. During those six years, he and Miriam spent much of their time in Japan, where they lived well as celebrities.

The project was a monumental engineering challenge for Wright. The site for the hotel consisted of 8 feet (2.4 meters) of surface soil riding on 60 to 70 feet (18 to 21 m) of soft mud. Tokyo often suffered from earthquakes. If an earthquake did strike, the ground would shake like a bowl of jelly. Remembering the collapse of Madison's capitol building, Wright was determined not to build a death trap.

Tokyo's frequent earth tremors drove Wright to revise countless plans. He later recalled being "sometimes wakened at night by strange sensations as at sea." The aftershocks, which heaved the earth upward and then back, gave Wright "a sense of the bottom falling from beneath the building." Wright pondered this wave movement and imagined a battleship at sea. "Why fight the quake?" he asked himself. "Why not sympathize with it and outwit it?"

A DIFFERENT KIND OF BUILDING

Wright decided to distribute the hotel's weight so that it "floated" on the mud below the hard ground. Boring into the site's soil and mud,

Happy in his Work

Wright was an early riser whose ideas often came as he worked on Taliesin's farm before breakfast. He designed buildings in his head while riding the road grader, directing the bulldozer, or walking the fields. Wright often came to the studio directly from the farm, bursting with new ideas.

At his work table, Wright focused intensely on detail after detail, boldly eliminating any that didn't fit the soul of his plan. He revised his drawings again and again, but he also took breaks to play Bach and Beethoven on the piano or to admire a piece from his collection of Japanese prints.

No matter how disordered his personal or professional life might have been, Frank Lloyd Wright was always a happy man in his studio, often humming tunes or telling jokes.

Wright made countless tests. He computed the weight and load of the building, pound by pound. The structure began to rise slowly upward from the site's layer of mud.

To ensure that the Imperial Hotel would be earthquake-proof, Wright made startling use of materials and introduced many innovations. His design included the following novel features:

- The floors of the building were mounted on pillars so they would move independently from the walls during an earthquake.

- Walls were wide at the bottom and became narrower at the top. These tapered walls had a lower center of gravity than traditional walls, minimizing the chance that they would topple.

- Pipes and wiring were laid in covered concrete trenches that were free of the structure. During an earthquake, they would not rip apart.

- Lightweight copper sheeting was used for the roof, instead of tiles. Falling roof tiles had killed thousands of people in earlier earthquakes.

- The hotel included a pool in its courtyard that could be used as a water source if fires broke out after an earthquake.

WILL IT WORK?

Wright always appeared unshakably confident about his designs. But he had taken a huge risk with his hotel plan. He had to defend himself against countless skeptics, especially as costs greatly exceeded original estimates. Then, in April, 1922, when the hotel was almost completed, a large earthquake shook Tokyo.

Later, Wright recalled being thrown to the ground by the impact. "As I lay there," he wrote, "I could clearly see the groundswell pass through the construction above as it heaved and groaned to hideous crashing and grinding noises." When he recovered and met with workers, he found the building to be undamaged. Soon after the earthquake, Frank returned to the United States with Miriam, leaving final work on the hotel to his assistants.

The Imperial Hotel. In his design, Wright sought to blend Western and Japanese elements. Although the hotel survived the devastating earthquake of 1923, it was demolished in 1968!

THE HOTEL SURVIVES!

On September 1, 1923, while Wright was working in Los Angeles, he heard shocking news. On the day set for the grand opening of the Imperial Hotel, the worst earthquake in Japan's history ravaged the cities of Tokyo and Yokohama. The earthquake ultimately resulted in 140,000 deaths and the destruction of 300,000 buildings.

In the days immediately following the earthquake, communications from Tokyo were cut off, and there was little news from the city. Newspaper executives repeatedly told Wright that the Imperial Hotel could not have survived. But twelve days after the earthquake, Wright received an astonishing cablegram from a Japanese official: HOTEL STANDS UNDAMAGED AS MONUMENT OF YOUR GENIUS. CONGRATULATIONS.

As word of the hotel's complete survival spread around the world, critics began to hail Wright as a genius and hero, and his reputation suddenly rocketed. In the fall of 1923, clients awed by the success of the Imperial Hotel flocked to Wright's office, asking for his services. For the first time in ten years, people seemed ready to forget the troubles of his personal life.

Hollyhock House

During the building of the Imperial Hotel, Wright also designed a huge home in Hollywood, California, for Aline Barnsdall, a rich **heir** to an oil fortune. When Hollyhock House was completed, many said it reminded them of a Mayan temple. Barnsdall and her daughter, Sugar Top, hardly ever lived in it, and she finally gave the entire property to the city of Los Angeles. Hollyhock House eventually became a famous public museum for children.

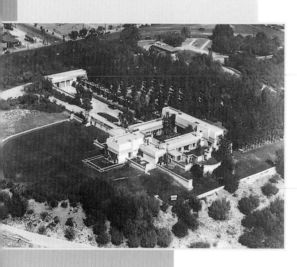

An aerial view of the Hollyhock House

In the fall of 1922, Catherine quietly agreed to grant Frank Wright the divorce he had wanted for twelve years. Frank and Miriam were married in November, but six months later, she left him and Taliesin. A year and a half later, he tried to divorce her. Miriam refused the divorce, and she also insisted to reporters that she had the right to live at Taliesin again.

By then, Wright had fallen in love with the beautiful young Olgivanna Hinzenberg, who had given birth to their daughter, Iovanna. Olgivanna, or "Olga," was still married to another man, with whom she also had a daughter, eight-year old Svetlana. At Taliesin, Frank lived with Olga, their baby Iovanna, and Svetlana. He was supervising another reconstruction of Taliesin, which had been struck by lightning and had burned again in April 1925. Wright told people that Olga was only his housekeeper, but he wasn't fooling anyone. More storm clouds were looming in his personal life.

Wright's tangled relationships with women created a monumental legal mess. When news reports revealed Miriam's fury over Wright's new affair, Olga's estranged husband tried to gain legal custody of Svetlana. Frank and Olga fled Wisconsin with the two children and hid in Minnesota. At the time, laws forbade a couple to cross state lines to live together without being married, and on October 21, 1926, authorities threw Frank and Olga in jail. Headlines across the nation broadcast reports of

Frank Lloyd Wright's newest scandal, which landed like a wrecking ball upon his newly flourishing career.

DOWN BUT NOT OUT

Frank and Olga were released from jail and reunited with the children, and Miriam finally agreed to financial terms for a divorce. But now Wright couldn't find clients. Huge legal bills, along with Taliesin mortgage payments and repairs, pushed Wright to the brink of financial ruin. A few devoted friends, family, and clients, however, formed a "rescue" corporation to save him. Philip La Follette, the young son of a famous Wisconsin governor and senator, led the corporation, which would take over and manage Wright's finances. Wright officially agreed to pay back his rescuers as he made money on future projects.

Frank Wright's third wife, Olgivanna, with their daughter, Iovanna

The bank evicted Frank, Olga, and the children from Taliesin. Fortunately, a family friend invited Wright to be a consultant on plans for a grand new resort hotel, the Arizona Biltmore, to built in Phoenix, Arizona. While the four spent a year in Arizona, La Follette painstakingly negotiated to bring Wright's finances and holdings under control. Finally, the newly married Frank and Olga Wright were able to come back to Taliesin.

NEW CHALLENGES

Although Wright's job prospects seemed dismal, two new projects appeared in early 1928. A wealthy Arizona real estate developer approached him regarding plans for another luxurious resort hotel. Then, in New York City, representatives of St. Marks-in-the-Bouwerie Church hired Wright to design several high-rise apartment buildings to be built as an investment. Wright eagerly plunged into work, producing a groundbreaking design.

TOUGH TIMES AGAIN

On October 29, 1929, the stock market crashed, ushering in the **Great Depression**. Wright's projects in New York evaporated, and he was left with no income. He was also unable to pay back the rescue corporation. Its members lost almost all of their money.

As the Great Depression became worse, Wright tried unsuccessfully to secure new commissions from various government offices. Despite the frightening outlook of his financial future, he was determined to remain visible in his field. He gave lectures at universities and wrote his autobiography. But his efforts produced little money and no architectural work.

By 1932, the Wrights were desperate. Frank sold some of his valuable Japanese art books. Olga wrote to Frank's sister, Maginel, begging for money. Wright was sixty-five years old, and most people thought his career as an architect was finished. But they had underestimated Frank Wright's remarkable ability to think creatively at the worst of times.

Luxuries Over Debts

As usual, Wright's renewed spirits sent him on a buying spree. Instead of focusing on paying back the people who had rescued him from financial disaster, he purchased four saddles and bridles for his horses at Taliesin, as well as expensive clothing and a new car.

Phil La Follette, who had not yet been paid a penny for his untiring efforts to help Wright, was stunned when he spotted Wright out for a spin in a brand new, bright orange car. Frank had purchased an L-29 Cord, a fast and very expensive automobile.

Recalling his unusual but exciting learning experience with Allan Conover in Madison, Wright decided to embark on a bold new project. At Taliesin, he would establish a school of architecture unlike any seen before.

Learning by doing would become the foundation of Wright's new school. Like Allen Conover, he would give his student apprentices experience in both drafting and on-site field work, such as carpentry, masonry, and construction supervision. Wright would also allow the students to help him with the commissions he received.

Frank Lloyd Wright with his students at Taliesin

Wright believed architects needed to be well-rounded people who appreciated the arts as he and Olga did. His students would become involved in music, visual arts, and drama, and they would also learn to plow a field and slop the pigs. The students would live at Taliesin and keep the farm running. They'd work in the kitchen, plant the food they ate, keep house, and regularly make repairs to Taliesin properties.

The new school was called the Taliesin Fellowship, and it attracted students much faster than Wright expected. By December 1932, thirty young men and women, from the United States and other countries, had enrolled and paid tuition.

As one of their first projects, Wright's students built a two-hundred-seat theater

Working or Playing?

Frank Lloyd Wright's students learned quickly that, despite his age, the famed architect was in excellent health and had a tireless zest for life. Wright loved variety in his day. He invented games, and he liked to give parties. Jack Howe, who became Wright's chief draftsman, recalled an important lesson he learned as an apprentice. "Mr. Wright played at working. He didn't do anything he didn't enjoy, but he enjoyed most everything."

Olgivanna, Fellowship Organizer

Olga was given charge of the Fellowship and was probably the secret of its success. She planned hefty meals and assigned all tasks, such as cooking, cleaning the chicken coop, and digging. Olgivanna could be stubborn and otherwise difficult to deal with, but she could also be generous, sympathetic, and helpful. Some people said she took care of Frank Wright as though he were a national treasure she had to protect.

at Taliesin. Opening the theater's doors to the public for films and other entertainment, Wright was able to draw patrons from Madison. The theater helped to offset the bad feelings Wright had caused by his scandals and outstanding bills.

The interior (above) and exterior (below) of Fallingwater

FALLINGWATER

Wright needed to bring in jobs for the Fellowship. But during the Great Depression of the 1930s, when one-fourth of workers in the United States were unemployed, architectural projects were almost impossible to find.

By happy coincidence, however, one of the Fellowship's first students was Edgar Kaufmann, Jr., whose father was a wealthy Pittsburgh department store owner. In 1934, the senior Kaufmann hired Wright to plan a number of civic projects. The Kaufmanns also asked Frank to build them a cottage in the country near a waterfall and ravine.

Later in life, Frank recalled the first time he saw the site. "There in a beautiful forest was a solid, high rock ledge rising beside a waterfall," he wrote, "and the natural thing seemed to be to cantilever the house from that rock bank over the falling water..."

In 1935, Frank Lloyd Wright's drawings created one of the most beautiful and famous houses in the world. The cantilevered struc-

The Drive that Made History

Frank Lloyd Wright liked to daydream about his projects and mull them over in his head before putting anything down on paper. But Edgar Kaufmann, Sr., grew impatient to see the cottage plans. While Kaufmann was visiting Milwaukee, he called Wright and unexpectedly announced that he was coming to Taliesin immediately. Wright calmly told Kaufmann that the drawings were finished. In fact, he hadn't even started them!

While Kaufmann drove the 140 miles (225 kilometers) from Milwaukee to Taliesin, Wright made architectural history at his drawing board. With his apprentices watching, Wright took three sheets of tracing paper—each in a different color, for the basement, first floor, and second floor—and began drawing furiously. He sketched in the plans for each floor, pouring out details onto the papers. Pencils wore down as fast as they could be sharpened. Wright talked about his drawings as he worked, so that his apprentices could learn. When he had finished his stunning plan, barely enough time remained for two apprentices to sketch views of the building. Wright presented one of these sketches to his client. Kaufmann's response? "Don't change a thing."

ture juts boldly over a waterfall. The design mirrors the surrounding rock outcroppings, which also became part of the interior. The house may be the best realization of Wright's idea that buildings should grow naturally from their surroundings. Wright named the enchanting home Fallingwater.

The main workroom of the Johnson building. Note the "lily pad" columns.

THE JOHNSON BUILDING

While he was producing plans for Fallingwater, Frank Lloyd Wright landed another commission that would increase his fame. S. C. Johnson & Son, Inc., the makers of a popular floor wax called Johnson's Wax, needed a new administration building in Racine, Wisconsin.

The building Wright designed gained worldwide admiration for the clean, modern lines of its exterior and its open interior, which included columns in the main workroom that resembled giant lily pads.

REALIZING A DIFFERENT GOAL

Although Wright enjoyed working on spectacular—and challenging—projects for wealthy clients, he had yet to accomplish a different, but no less ambitious, goal. Wright wanted to build a house for people with modest incomes, one that would cost $5,000. In his view, affordable houses were essential to the democratic way of life in the United States.

Wright decided that the Taliesin Fellowship would make a major effort to produce lower-cost homes. The Fellowship began the first of these houses in Madison in June 1937, for Herb and Katherine Jacobs. The budget was a strict $5,500. Although such a low-cost project would not bring a lot of money, Wright gave it an extraordinary amount of attention, producing seventy drawings as he drafted designs.

THE USONIAN HOUSE

The Jacobs project became a **prototype** for an entirely new style of dwelling that Wright named the Usonian house. (The name was derived from "United States of North America.") He was dedicated to constructing a solid, quality house with many new features, but he used every means possible to keep down the cost of labor and materials.

The Usonian house reflected some of the Prairie Style's principles. It had a wide, overhanging roof, a fireplace, and an open living room-dining room area. But the Usonian house also offered many new, modern features. The single-story structure was heated through the floor, with hot-water pipes set in gravel under a concrete slab. Both the kitchen and laundry were close to the living areas. Carefully designed windows and doors admitted natural light and provided a sense of the house's setting.

When the Jacobs House was finished, in 1936, it brought a flood of visitors. People marveled at its trend-setting features, and then they flocked to Wright for their own house plans. These potential homeowners ran into problems, however, when they submitted the plans to city planning boards or to banks where they were asking for loans. Officials doubted the walls would support the roof and claimed that floor heating wasn't practical. Nevertheless, about 140 Usonian houses were built, and countless American homes were ultimately influenced by Usonian ideas.

A view of the back side of Jacobs House, in Madison, Wisconsin. While the front of the house has small windows to provide protection from street noise, the back of the house has large windows that offer views of the natural world outside. Note the house's wide roof overhangs.

Proving the Skeptics Wrong

When Albert and Edie Adleman of Fox Point, Wisconsin, submitted Wright's plan for their house to the city planning board, it was rejected. "The city said the roof wouldn't do," Adleman explained. "Wright had to appear and convince them from an engineering point of view that the **angle iron** support in the living room would hold the thirty foot roof span and a load of snow." Wright's argument convinced the city officials, and they approved the plan. "In fifty-five years," Adleman said, "we've never had a problem."

CHAPTER 7

A CREATIVE LIFE CONTINUES

Buildings such as the Jacobs House, the Johnson headquarters, and Fallingwater attracted national publicity. Taliesin became a tourist attraction, and Wright completed several profitable projects. He was able to produce an astonishing number of highly original designs, largely with the help of his students. The Taliesin Fellowship—another example of Wright's genius for thinking "outside the box"—continued to draw students from all over the world.

Center of Attention

Wright was an excellent, if egotistical, teacher. For him, the more people who gathered to watch and listen while he sat at his drafting table, the better. Wesley Peters, who married Olgivanna's daughter, Svetlana, said Wright "had so much life and energy; it shaped everyone around him." Wright genuinely cared for his students and wanted them to learn. But he also feared competition, and he resented students whose work he considered to be *too* good.

Wesley Peters (left) and Frank Lloyd Wright

TALIESIN GROWS

As Wright prospered, he bought properties surrounding Taliesin instead of paying back old debts. Over a thirty-year span, Taliesin grew to 3,000 acres (1,214 hectares) and came to include 3 miles (4.8 km) of beautiful waterfront on the Wisconsin River.

Wright also bought land outside Scottsdale, Arizona. After a nasty bout of pneumonia, and with Olga's urging, he decided to flee Wisconsin's harsh winters. Moving the Fellowship temporarily to the Arizona desert, he directed construction of Taliesin West while the apprentices lived in tents.

To keep rooms cool during the day but warmer at night, Wright designed massive slanting walls made of a mix of cement and desert rock. Redwood rafters topped the walls. Canvas-covered openings allowed airflow and filtered sunlight inside. The finished building fit into the landscape and offered dazzling views. Even in the hostile desert, Wright had produced a comfortable, inspiring environment.

When Taliesin West was livable, the Fellowship began operating in Wisconsin during the warm months of the year and in Arizona during the winter.

Taliesin West. The building's sharp-edged rock walls help it blend in with the landscape.

The interior of Taliesin West

MORE HEARTBREAK, MORE WORK

In 1946, a terrible tragedy struck the Taliesin community. Olga's daughter Svetlana, the popular wife of Wesley Peters, was killed in an automobile accident, along with one of the couple's two young sons. The deaths had an impact on everyone at Taliesin, and Olga's grief caused her to sink into months of depression. At the time, Wright was almost eighty years

Truth Against the World

By the late 1930s, Wright had become a national celebrity, and he used this role to express his opinion on any and every subject. He adopted the motto of his mother's family—"Truth Against the World." Wright deeply believed in democracy and the American way of life, but he became known for his attacks on U.S. politics and economic policies. He always sided with the most liberal thinking and was outspoken in his views against war. During World War II (1939–1945), the Federal Bureau of Investigation (FBI) was on the lookout for traitors and spies, and Wright's antiwar statements made him a suspect. He was investigated but never charged with any crimes.

The interior of the Guggenheim Museum. Spiraling floors wind around a large courtyard that is topped with a skylight.

old. But he believed new work would heal the grieving Taliesin community.

Commissions still poured into the Fellowship. In 1949 and 1950, more than forty houses and other buildings were completed. Their locations across the country were proof of the widespread popularity of Frank Lloyd Wright's designs. Wright had become so famous that taxi drivers and waiters were said to recognize him.

THE GUGGENHEIM MUSEUM

In 1943, at age seventy-six, Wright signed a contract to design the Guggenheim Museum, his first project in New York City. Wright imagined visitors to the museum moving without interruption through a circular gallery space. Inventing a practical and acceptable design for this unusual concept became a long struggle—sixteen years of criticism, building code negotiations, and revision demands, with the usual soaring costs.

Wright's astonishing structure was finally constructed in 1959. The Guggenheim Museum's snail-like form has no separate floor levels. Instead, it leads visitors on a continuous spiral as they view artwork, as though they are strolling up or down a gentle slope. Today, the structure designed to showcase artists' work is now considered a work of art in its own right.

"A Contribution to My Boyhood Home"

Throughout Wright's professional life, he longed to design a major public building in his boyhood home of Madison. In 1938, when Wright was seventy-one years old, he submitted a brilliant proposal for a new civic center along Lake Monona. Opponents argued fiercely that Wright was an unfit role model to represent the city of Madison.

During the last twenty-one years of his life, Wright tried to satisfy Madison officials, producing four thousand sheets of sketches, one thousand pages of specifications, and eight separate designs. In 1953, at age eighty-six, he publicly appealed to the people of Madison. "I'm just an old fool who would like to make a final contribution to my boyhood home," he said.

For more than thirty years after Wright's death, hearings, legal battles, and revisions of his plans continued. When construction of Monona Terrace finally began, in 1994, the spirit of Wright's vision remained, although many changes had taken place. *Time* magazine reported that the groundbreaking ceremony honored "the most important Wright-designed project never executed in his lifetime." The building opened in 1997 (see photo on p. 7).

A LONG, FULL LIFE

Frank Lloyd Wright is proof that creative thinking knows no age limit. Even as he approached ninety years of age, he was still showing the world how to use fresh and ingenious approaches to architectural challenges.

Residents of Taliesin were making plans for Frank's ninety-second birthday when they received word that he had been taken to the hospital for an operation. He would never return. On Thursday, April 9, 1959, Frank Wright died. Despite his advanced age, Wright's death shocked many people, who had expected him to rise from yet another crisis. But Frank Lloyd Wright's long, full life had finally come to an end.

The funeral procession for Frank Lloyd Wright passes in front of his home at Taliesin.

TIMELINE

1867	Frank Lloyd Wright is born on June 7 in Richland Center, Wisconsin
1877	The Wright family settles in Madison, Wisconsin, on the shore of Lake Mendota
1878	Frank spends his first of six summers working on his uncle James's farm near Spring Green, Wisconsin
1883	Witnesses devastation from the collapsed wing of the Capitol building in Madison
1886	Hired by Allen Conover. Also enrolls as a part-time student at the University of Wisconsin in Madison
1887	Leaves Madison for Chicago, Illinois, and works for J. L. Silsbee
1888	Hired by Chicago architectural firm Adler and Sullivan
1889	Marries Catherine Lee Tobin
1903	Breakthrough design for the Larkin Company administration building is constructed in Buffalo, New York
1910	Prairie house in Chicago for Frederick C. Robie is completed
1911	Construction begins on Taliesin, near Spring Green
1914	Mamah Cheney, her two children and four others are killed, and Taliesin is set afire by a crazed handyman
1923	An earthquake destroys most of Tokyo, Japan, but the Wright-designed Imperial Hotel survives, bringing Wright world fame
1929	The stock market crashes, and Wright's clients are lost
1932	The Taliesin Fellowship is founded, and students enroll
1935	Fallingwater is built in Bear Run, Pennsylvania
1936	Johnson administration building is built in Racine, Wisconsin
1937	Construction begins on the Jacobs Usonian House in Madison, Wisconsin, and Taliesin West near Scottsdale, Arizona
1943	Wright is commissioned to design the Guggenheim Art Museum
1959	Wright dies on April 9 in Arizona. Funeral services are held at Taliesin in Wisconsin

GLOSSARY

angle iron: a piece of iron or steel in the shape of an "L" that joins structures together at an angle.

autobiography: an account of a person's life written by that person.

classical: relating to ancient Greece or Rome.

commissions: formal, written orders to perform a particular work.

delegated: entrusted to another person.

girders: large beams used in buildings, made of wood, metal, or concrete.

graphic arts: the various arts involved in printing and publishing, such as engraving, etching, and photography.

Great Depression: a severe economic slump during the 1930s, when many people in the United States and other countries lost their jobs and savings.

heir: a person who inherits wealth.

lime: a substance used to make mortar (which holds together bricks) and plaster.

mink: an animal fur prized for its softness.

moonlight: hold two or more jobs at once.

negligence: a lack of proper care and attention to a particular job or activity.

pawn shop: a business that loans money in exchange for something of value that it holds until the loan is repaid.

prairies: large, open areas of level or rolling grassland.

prototype: a design that serves as the basis for subsequent designs.

sacrilege: the harming or disrespecting of something considered sacred, such as a church.

skylights: windows in roofs that let in natural light.

strata: layers of rock or earth.

tuition: the fee that a school requires for providing an education.

Welsh: having to do with Wales, which is part of Great Britain.

Victorian: relating to the era of Queen Victoria of Great Britain, who reigned from 1837 to 1901.

TO FIND OUT MORE

BOOKS

Davis, Frances A. *Frank Lloyd Wright: Maverick Architect.* Minneapolis: Lerner Publications, 1996.

Middleton, Haydn. *Frank Lloyd Wright (Creative Lives).* Crystal Lake, Ill.: Heinemann Library, 2001.

Rubin, Susan Goldman. *Frank Lloyd Wright (First Impressions).* New York: Abrams Books for Young Readers, 1994.

Thorne-Thomsen, Kathleen and Sabbeth, Carol. *Frank Lloyd Wright for Kids: His Life and Ideas.* Chicago: Chicago Review Press, 1994.

Wright, David K. *Frank Lloyd Wright: Visionary Architect (People to Know).* Berkeley Heights, N.J.: Enslow, 1999.

INTERNET SITES

Wright on the Web
www.delmars.com/wright/flw2.htm
A biography of Wright and many good photos of Wright buildings.

All-Wright Site, An Internet Guide to Frank Lloyd Wright
www.geocities.com/SoHo/1469/flw.html
Links to many internet sites about Wright.

The Frank Lloyd Wright Foundation
www.franklloydwright.org
History of Wright and the Taliesin Fellowship.

The Life and Work of Frank Lloyd Wright
www.pbs.org/flw/buildings/index.html.
A PBS web site offering drawings, photos, and histories of many important buildings designed by Wright.

Fallingwater
www.GreatBuildings.com/buildings/Fallingwater.html
Great photos and comments about the most famous house designed by Wright.

INDEX *(continued)*

About the Author

Gretchen Will Mayo says writing biographies resembles writing mysteries. "I lift layers of information, one by one, to dig ever closer to the subject's heart, always attempting to answer the question, 'What caused this heart to beat faster?' I wanted to know what made Frank Lloyd Wright behave and choose in ways that set him apart." Ms. Mayo has published many fiction and nonfiction books for children. She is also a teacher and illustrator. From Vermont College, she earned her Masters in Fine Arts in Writing for Children. She and her husband are Wisconsinites, living in a house greatly influenced by Frank Lloyd Wright's ideas. From every room, nature can be viewed and enjoyed.